An opinionated guide to

INDEPENDENT
LONDON

T0124505

Written by
IMOGEN LEPERE

Photography by
LESLEY LAU

The Cloth Shop (no.23)

INFORMATION IS DEAD.
LONG LIVE OPINION.

With the virus in our midst and the internet our escape, what is the point of a book about the best independent shops in London?

Well, precisely because they are that: independent and oh-so-real. These shops are unique, curated, deeply personal, and yes, you can actually touch them. In a time of social distance and online shopping, going out to these havens of taste is not only satisfying, it's socially important.

The guide books in this series give our unashamed opinion about the best places to visit in London. Information is easy to come by. Reliable opinion with original photography is more precious.

Ann and Martin
Founders, Hoxton Mini Press

Other books in the series:

Labour and Wait (no.36)

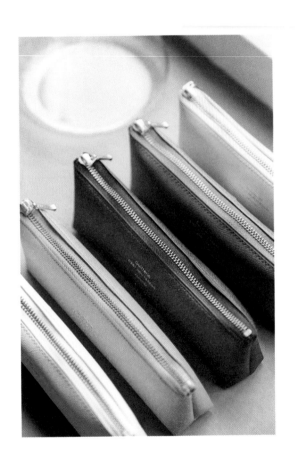

Present and Correct (no.3)
Opposite: A New Tribe (no.39)

CONTRIBUTORS

Imogen Lepere is a Brixton-born, Hackney Wick-based journalist specialising in the quirkier side of travel. She has a weakness for stories of little people standing up to the system and found the owners of these shops so inspiring she ended up blowing most of her paycheck while visiting them. All in the name of research…

Hong Kong-born photographer *Lesley Lau* began her career in the City before discovering she was more interested in shutter speeds than share prices. For this book, she cycled more than 200 miles with her kit strapped to her bike. She'd happily peddle the same again if it meant supporting small, independent businesses.

Hoxton Mini Press is a small indie publisher based in east London. We make books about London – we love and breathe this city – and always with a dedication to good photography and lovely production. When we started the company people told us print was dead. That inspired us. Books are no longer about information but objects in their own right: something to collect and own and inspire.

INTRODUCTION

Above the beat of Britpop and groans of construction coming from the site that would soon become Canary Wharf, another sound defined the 90s: the death rattle of the British high street. Or so cynics thought.

During the decade, rising rents in cities resulted in an invasion of out-of-town shopping centres such as Bluewater and Lakeside. Amazon and eBay both launched in 1995, introducing us to the convenience of purchasing in our PJs. The early 00s also saw the rise of behemoths such as Primark, which peddled mass consumerism at prices so low it seemed there must have been some kind of mistake.

But in recent years, as buyers move away from the mass-produced and become more aware of supporting their local community, independent shops have staged something of a comeback. Many have drawn inspiration from retail in the first half of the 20th century – a gentler time when owners knew the names of their customers' children and most of the stock was locally made.

Supporting independent shops rather than chains is more sustainable in the most holistic sense of the word. As Mariam Tijani of African concept store Bidhaar (no.22) reminded me, objects don't just appear out of nowhere. Every item has a knock-on effect, both in terms of the environment and the lives of the people who make them. Shopping independently is a shortcut to spending more responsibly – quite literally putting your money where your mouth is. As buyers in an increasingly time-poor world, we don't have time to research every purchase and decide if it fits with our values. In independent shops, someone we trust has done that work for us.

An independent shop is the physical embodiment of the owners' passions. The proprietor has often chosen every item and can tell you the story behind each one. With such detailed knowledge, they are in a position to offer expert advice. Looking for a material that's tough enough to withstand rain but still feels soft on bare skin? Ask Susie Harley of The Cloth Shop (no.23). With such encyclopaedic knowledge, owners often act as consultants for emerging talent in their field too. Simon Alderson and Tony Cunningham, of Twentytwentyone (no.53), have mentored countless young British designers.

Independent shops are also integral to the health of London's creative scene. Without these commercial platforms, how could ceramicists keep their wheels turning or illustrators justify the cost of their ink? Other shops act as guardians of disappearing British crafts. Rachel Wythe-Moran and Simon Watkins of Labour and Wait (no.36) are personally responsible for protecting Guernsey jumpers, those thick, fibrous garments that have been a favourite with fishermen for 300 years. There are only three craftspeople who still hand loom them the traditional way and the shop has pledged to buy enough stock to keep them in business for as long as it remains open.

And not all heritage is tangible. Floris (no.25) and Berry Bros & Rudd (no.24) have been stolid depositories for the everyday stories of generations of Londoners for hundreds of years. These shops hold memories in their bricks and mortar. To splash Floris' Limes scent on your wrist is to connect with London's past in a more visceral way than could ever be experienced at a museum.

The truth is that our credit card histories provide a far more realistic insight into our day to day existence than our Instagram feeds. The coffees slurped on sluggish mornings, the outfit before a date and the furniture that turns a new house into a home are vignettes that make up the narrative of our lives. When I asked jeweller Jos Skeates of E.C. One (no.12) what he enjoys most about his work, he replied 'the privilege of meeting people at pivotal moments'. Although he specialises in engagement rings, his favourite piece is a pendant with a lost love's hair concealed behind a precious stone. It seems that sometimes physical objects can say the things we struggle to put into words.

Of course, it would be impossible not to mention the effects of the Coronavirus pandemic. When beginning work on this collection at the start of UK lockdown in March 2020, the Hoxton Mini Press team feared that some shops would not survive. All but one on the original list have. Owners spoke emotionally about the overwhelming support they received in the form of emails, donations and visits from regulars, despite the fact many were facing financial uncertainty themselves.

Proof, if ever we heard it, that independent shops are so much more valuable than the sum of their stock.

Inogen Lepere
London, 2020

1

L. CORNELISSEN & SON

Celebrated art supplies in a storied setting

Head to London's most picturesque art shop and browse for paints alongside signwriters picking up sheets of gold leaf, icon painters stocking up on squirrel brushes and pastel makers comparing resins. In the art world, Cornelissen's has been known for selling the best supplies on the market since 1855. Intriguing mahogany drawers are begging to be opened and glass jars of 'tartrazine yellow' and 'Venetian red' pigments will have you feeling like a kid in a sweet shop – even if your art skills don't extend beyond colouring in. It's a few minutes' walk from the British Museum too.

105 Great Russell Street, WC1B 3RY
Nearest station: Tottenham Court Road
cornelissen.com @l.cornelissen_and_son

2

PENTREATH & HALL

Forward-thinking homewares inspired by the past

'Good things for the home' is how Ben Pentreath and Bridie Hall describe their interiors shop, which is just off always-chic Lamb's Conduit Street (and near Persephone Books, see no.4). Ben, an architect, and artist Bridie find endless inspiration in their love of jewel-bright colours and classical history. Their own-design stationery, informed by the floors of St Mark's Basilica, is displayed alongside candlesticks in the shape of ionic columns and a host of quirky gems from lesser-known British designers. A small but perfectly formed selection of antiques including Wedgwood and Staffordshire porcelain introduce the traditions of the British country house to a new generation.

17 Rugby Street, WC1N 3QT
Nearest station: Russell Square
pentreath-hall.com @pentreathandhall

3

PRESENT AND CORRECT

*Vintage and new stationery with
an international flavour*

This immaculate stationery hub has an enormous Insta following and it's not hard to see why. Not so much as a single vintage paper clip is out of place. Owner Neal Whittington worked as a graphic designer for *Monocle* and has a killer eye for mid-century typography. The stock comes from flea markets and small makers in more than 18 countries. Every item is hand-picked by him, making it feel like the collection of that arty student in school you secretly envied. Don't miss the nostalgic vending machine in the corner, which dispenses cute mystery capsules for just £2.

*23 Arlington Way, EC1R 1UY
Nearest station: Angel
presentandcorrect.com @presentandcorrect*

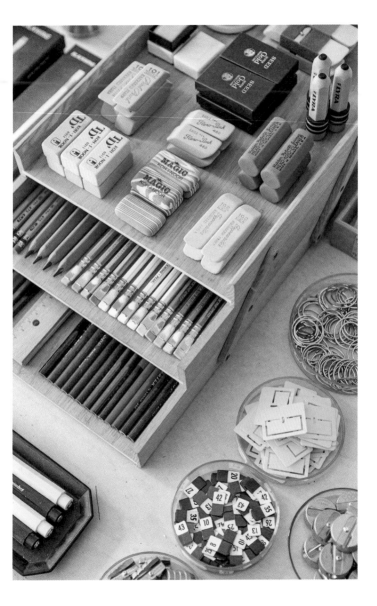

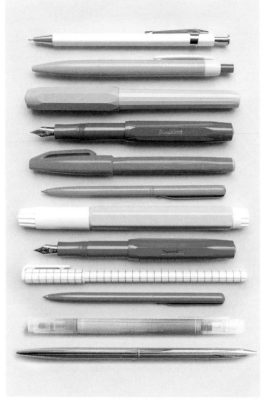

4

PERSEPHONE BOOKS

*Publishing house championing forgotten
female authors*

With its muted lighting, Thonet chairs and squeaky
floorboards, Persephone has the atmosphere of a lady
author's parlour in the 1930s. Nicola Beauman founded
the press in 1999 to give overlooked female writers
of the early 20th century the recognition they deserve
and has since brought to light names such as Dorothy
Whipple and Winifred Watson. Every title has an elegant
grey cover and endpapers printed with a fabric design
from the year it was first published. As if supporting
female artists wasn't reason enough to visit, Lamb's
Conduit Steet is the heart of Clerkenwell's design
district and jam-packed with independent shops.

*59 Lamb's Conduit Street, WC1N 3NB
Nearest station: Russell Square
persephonebooks.co.uk @persephonebooks*

5

JAMES SMITH & SONS UMBRELLAS

Heritage umbrellas, crafted on site

Part umbrella purveyor, part legend, this shop has been a London landmark since 1830. The owner, the fifth generation of the founding family, still works on the shop floor although prefers to go incognito. Just three times a day a bell tinkles from the subterranean workshop, letting the serving staff know that another bespoke umbrella is ready. The shop itself is filled with curios the founder's son, also called James Smith, collected on his travels, all of which are for sale. Think a Polynesian fertility stick and horns from long-extinct animals. It's as charming as it is eccentric – and more authentically London than Dickens and David Bowie combined.

53 New Oxford Street, WC1A 1BL
Nearest station: Tottenham Court Road
james-smith.co.uk @jamessmithandsons

6

BENJAMIN POLLOCK'S TOYSHOP

Traditional toys inspired by London's theatres

Established by Mr Pollock in 1880, this eclectic spot was the first permanent shop to open in Covent Garden Market – and the last of the originals to survive. Its dragon's-blood carpets nod to its location in the heart of the West End and a star-studded cast of regulars includes Emma Thompson and Joanna Lumley. The stock could have been plucked from your grandma's toy chest: shadow boxes to be coloured in, kaleidoscopes and wind-up music boxes. Swap your Christmas charades session for an evening spent making one of their slot together toy theatres, which are handcrafted in Italy and come with a cast of Victorian characters.

44 The Market, WC2E 8RF
Nearest station: Covent Garden
pollocks-coventgarden.co.uk
@benjamin_pollocks_toyshop

7

ALGERIAN COFFEE STORES

A family-run Soho stalwart for coffee lovers

Follow the smell of coffee to one of the last bastions of old Soho and the only surviving independent shop on Old Compton Street. Inside it's as animated as an auction house, with staff scurrying up ladders to scoop 80 coffees and more than 120 teas out of glass jars. Fittings date back to 1887 and the customer service is equally traditional. Sisters Daniela and Marisa are the third generation of the Crocetta family to run the shop. They've given countless Baby Boomers, Generation Xers and Millennials their caffeine-fix. If the prices stay this reasonable (cappuccino for £1.20), they'll probably sell to Gen Z's children too.

52 Old Compton Street, W1D 4PB
Nearest station: Piccadilly Circus
algeriancoffeestores.com @algerian_coffee_stores

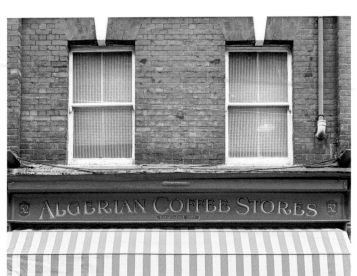

8

CHOOSING KEEPING

A homage to artisan stationery and crafts

When you think back to your childhood, it's the little things you remember most: the fountain pen on your grandfather's desk, the Japanese Nori glue you used in art class. This highly specialised stationery shop prompts these memories by stocking nostalgic products made traditionally by artisans in France, Germany, Italy and the UK. Owner Julia Jeuvell believes that thoughtfully designed everyday things – from Bic biros to steel scissors – have cultural significance and deserve to be celebrated. After spending a few minutes browsing, we think you'll agree with her.

21 Tower Street, WC2H 9NS
Nearest station: Leicester Square
choosingkeeping.com @choosingkeeping

9

BOTANIQUE WORKSHOP

Whimsical lifestyle shop specialising in the handmade

If Etsy had a real-life shop, it would look like this. From dried rose headbands to soy wax candles, owner Alice Howard crafts many of the products herself, with the others sourced from small, equally passionate makers. Don't miss the opportunity to stock up on natural detergents and eco-friendly shampoos in the zero-waste room, as well as freshly-cut blooms from the flower stall outside. A cuddle with shop pups Goose and Bertie is strongly recommended.

31 Exmouth Market, EC1R 4QL
Nearest station: Farringdon
botaniqueworkshop.com @botaniqueworkshop

10

THE SCHOOL OF LIFE

Emotional tools to help you live your best life

Love, work, mental health – there are plenty of situations school didn't equip us to navigate; consider this organisation the wise headteacher you wish you'd had. Founded by philosopher and author Alain de Botton, it aims to help people find calm, self-understanding, resilience and connection. Their Marchmont Street site is part bookshop and part classroom, where trained psychotherapists hold regular workshops. Browse their full range of beautifully designed books, cards and therapeutic products before having conversations about things that really matter with like-minded souls.

70 Marchmont Street, WC1N 1AB
Nearest station: Russell Square
theschooloflife.com @theschooloflifelondon

11

MAGCULTURE

A temple to indie magazines

This shop is the boss of London's print scene. Take a
seat on one of the leather sofas and flick through more
than 500 publications from 20 countries, including
founder Jeremy Leslie's favourites: *It's Freezing in LA*,
Here and *Pin-Up*. Jeremy started as a designer for *Time
Out* and *The Guardian* and personally chooses every
title; only those that offer something truly unique in
content or design pass his litmus test. You'll find the
shop in London's first purpose-built tower block: a
striking modernist building that has plenty of interest
in its own right.

270 St John Street, EC1V 4PE
Nearest Station: Farringdon
magculture.com @magculture

12

E.C. ONE

Sustainable jeweller specialising in
bespoke engagement rings

This gem offers all the personalised service of a Savile Row tailor's shop. Owner Jos Skeates did his first apprenticeship at the age of 16 and is now a Master Goldsmith. In an open studio at the back, four more goldsmiths craft their magic under his watchful eye. At the front, their creations are displayed alongside 30 mostly young designers, including Flora Battachari. Co-owner and buyer Alison Skeates has a magpie's eye for unusual gems (champagne diamonds, pink sapphires). The clincher? All their treasures are made sustainably, with ethically sourced jewels and recycled metal.

41 Exmouth Market, EC1R 4QL
Nearest station: Farringdon
econe.co.uk @econe_jewellery

13

IYOUALL

Leading-edge design studio and homewares

This design studio and lifestyle store more than plays its part in confirming East Dulwich as one of south London's most sought-after villages. Owners Fleur Patterson and partner Matt Cottis count Folk among their major clients and their two-floor showroom is infused with simple Scandi style. Downstairs, find furniture from brands such as Ferm Living, MENU, HAY and Normann Copenhagen. Upstairs is a stationery and homewares hub stocking local makers and overseas artists who may otherwise struggle to get distribution. Look out for Pipkin and Co's soy candles and By Obie's whimsical wooden figures, carved by hand in Indonesia.

48 East Dulwich Road, SE22 9AX
Nearest station: East Dulwich
Other locations: Deptford, King's Cross
iyouall.com @iyouallstore

14

MONS CHEESEMONGERS

High-end fromage from a family of affineurs

With their bowties and walrus moustaches the Mons brothers look like they've just strolled out of a bistro on Paris' Left Bank. Gooey bries, creamy camemberts and crumbling cigars of goat cheese are piled high on the counter, while staff wearing tasteful linen aprons restock shelves with quality sundries. Products are matured until perfectly ripe in caves owned by their father in Auvergne, or in their dedicated Bermondsey warehouse. Prices may be more suited to boards at sophisticated soirées than comforting toasties, but more than 60 years of affineur knowledge is well worth shelling out for.

153 Lordship Lane, SE22 8HX
Nearest station: East Dulwich
Other locations: Bermondsey, Borough
mons-cheese.co.uk @monscheeseuk

15

THE BOOK AND RECORD BAR

A hidden gem for anyone who's serious about music

One of south London's best-stocked community record shops hides in the sleepy residential streets between West Norwood and Crystal Palace. But that's kind of the point. With little passing trade, this shop survives by serving serious collectors and professional DJs on the hunt for hard-to-get 90s dance tracks and 60s psychedelia. Most afternoons decks are set up and the courtyard fills with music lovers sharing tips, coffee and local craft beer. They also have their own pirate radio station, WNBC.

20 Norwood High Street, SE27 9NR
Nearest station: West Norwood
bookandrecordbar.co.uk @thebookandrecordbar

17

GENERAL STORE

Peckham grocer with a passion for provenance

Equal parts nostalgia and contemporary finesse, this charcoal-painted grocer would put Nigella's larder to shame. The dedication to provenance borders on obsessive and for the most part prices are fully justified by quality (although ceramic pomegranates for £25 may be a step too far.) Order a Workshop coffee – and one of London's best pastel de natas, if you're early enough – to enjoy on the benches outside, as Bellenden Road locals amble by. Note: the cast iron bollards along the street by sculptor Antony Gormley bear a suspicious resemblance to adult toys.

174 Bellenden Road, SE15 4BW
Nearest station: Peckham Rye
generalsto.re @general_store

18

LONDON TERRARIUMS

Miniature gardens in glass bottles

When Emma Sibley started making terrariums in 2015, they were still a kooky piece of Victoriana. Now you can barely open Pinterest without seeing one of these tiny glass gardens. Part studio, part shop, her cactus-filled New Cross pad is the stuff of millennial dreams. Browse botanical books, succulents and chic gardening accessories such as watering cans and misters. She also holds regular workshops where green-fingered types can build their own – although this is not a skill for the impatient. Plan ahead because the shop only opens on weekends.

106a New Cross Road, SE14 5BA
Nearest station: New Cross
Other location: Inside Heal's, Tottenham Court Road
londonterrariums.com @londonterrariums

19

FOREST

An Eden of plants and lifestyle luxuries

This picturesque plant shop will have even the most diehard urbanites reaching for their watering cans – and cameras. A canopy of plants trails from metal girders, Asian ceramics balance on rustic crates and jungle climbers creep from concrete pots. The uncompromising taste of mother-daughter owners Fran and Alice Bailey is demonstrated further by a scattering of drool-worthy homewares and toiletries. Aromatic body balms and pet shampoos will have you and your pooch smelling of roses in no time.

43 Lordship Lane, SE22 8EW
Nearest station: East Dulwich
Other location: Deptford
forest.london @forest_london

20

LASSCO

Architectural salvage and antiques
in a living museum

Step off Vauxhall's A21 roundabout into the lost world of this Georgian villa. Its National Trust feel is down to the fact that much of it has been magpied from historic buildings around London. Railings from St Paul's Cathedral, a winged fireplace from Alexander McQueen's flagship store and the golden columns Versace created for the Sultan of Brunei's Chelsea mansion: every object has a tale to tell. Owner Adrian Amos has more than 40 years' experience and his web of contacts is second to none. If he can't track down that rare Edwardian handle, you can be pretty sure it no longer exists.

30 Wandsworth Road, sw8 2LG
Nearest station: Vauxhall
Other location: Bermondsey
lassco.co.uk @lasscobrunswickhouse

21

GIDDY GROCER

Fine British foods and farm-fresh produce

This shop's ethos is to keep the provenance as local as possible and products such as Pao's kimchi, Spring bone broth and Mirko's vegan cheese are all made by Bermondsey residents. Loiter here for long enough and you'll probably see one of them delivering their goods by bicycle. Owner Chris Hall's grandparents ran a grocery store in the New Forest and this heritage can be felt in the antique dresser, marble cheese counter and freshly scrawled chalkboards. With Borough and Maltby Street food markets within a 10-minute stroll, this shop needs to be on top of its game. It won't disappoint.

80 Bermondsey Street, SE1 3UD
Nearest station: London Bridge
giddygrocer.co.uk @giddygrocer

22

BIDHAAR

Concept store dedicated to African talent

Nigerian-born Mariam Tijani is on a mission to give contemporary African creatives the recognition they deserve in the UK. Her Peckham Market shop is an incubator for creative talent from her motherland, and around 50% of the stock is handmade: grandad shirts in hand-dyed batik, wicker bags from Cameroon and sleek blazers of aso oke, the traditional fabric of the Yoruba people. Mariam designs some items herself, while other labels include Congolese cushion brand Duarra and Lagoniassa. When it comes to supporting the next generation of African talent, this shop is doing real work – and making it look seriously stylish in the process.

Ground Floor Market, 133A Rye Lane, SE15 4BQ
Nearest station: Peckham Rye
bidhaar.com @bidhaarofficial

23

THE CLOTH SHOP

Sustainable fabrics and antique table linens

What makes The Cloth Shop a Portobello must? For a start, they stock more than 150 types of organic linen: whether looking for upholstery twill or something for summer overalls, they've got you covered. Their fabrics, from Irish tweed to Khadi silks, are made from predominantly natural materials. And then there's the Harley family themselves; both founders' grandparents worked in fashion and Sam and wife Susie have nearly 30 years of drapery knowledge in their own right. Their son Henry, who now manages the shop, started working here when he was 13, so you couldn't be in more experienced and enthusiastic hands.

290 Portobello Road, W10 5TE
Nearest station: Westbourne Park
theclothshop.net @clothshoplondon

24

BERRY BROS & RUDD

Eighth-generation wine merchant
that improves with age

Follow in the footsteps of Beau Brummel, Lord Byron
and pretty much every other Regency dandy to
London's most eminent wine shop. Interiors have
barely changed since first opening in St James's in
1698 – except of course the temperature-controlled
section where the fine wines are stored. Browse
old favourites and future classics as well as curios
like The King's Ginger, a heady liqueur formulated
especially for King Edward VII. Think this all sounds
a little exclusive? The highly educated team love
sharing their knowledge and the bestseller is an easy-
drinking claret that's £11 a bottle.

63 Pall Mall, SW1Y 5HZ
Nearest station: Green Park
bbr.com @berrybrosrudd

PRIVATE

25

FLORIS

Quintessentially British family-run perfumers

Floris' signature fragrance, 'Limes', was created to cut through the odours of 18th-century London; it works just as well at rush hour on the Piccadilly line today. The oldest shop on Jermyn Street and run by the ninth generation of the founding family, Floris is a true time warp, with mahogany display cabinets sourced from the Great Exhibition in 1851. In the on-site workshop you can watch artisans hand-pouring perfume using antique instruments and the original formula books. Past Floris fans were an illustrious crowd: Marilyn Monroe cheated on Chanel with six bottles of Rose Geranium, while Churchill wore Special 127.

89 Jermyn Street, SW1Y 6JH
Nearest station: Green Park
florislondon.com @florislondon

26

COUVERTURE & THE GARBSTORE

A stylish union of homeware and casualwear

When Emily Dyson-Paley (of homewares brand Couverture) married Ian Paley (founder of chic menswear label The Garbstore) one of London's best concept stores was born. Housed in a townhouse that was once a timber yard, it channels the bohemian spirit of nearby Portobello Market through three-floors of emerging and independent labels from all over the world. The interior is a mix of old and new with Portuguese tiles and an antique brass porter's trolley used as a display cabinet. Like its Notting Hill postcode, this shop never seems to go out of style.

188 Kensington Park Road, W11 2ES
Nearest station: Ladbroke Grove
couvertureandthegarbstore.com
@couverture @garbstore

27

ANOTHER COUNTRY

*Contemporary furniture and fittings made
from sustainable timber*

There's something effortlessly pleasing about Another
Country's furniture, which draws inspiration from
Japanese, Scandinavian and Shaker aesthetics and
is made in their own workshop in Portugal. Their
signature items are elevated versions of design classics:
oak rockers inspired by 19th-century chairs and ash
chests with brass detailing. Owner Paul de Zwart
published *Wallpaper** for many years and his vision
for your home is as sleek as the magazine itself. If
space is an issue, you can take home a slice of the
lifestyle through tasteful accessories: an oiled walnut
pencil pot will leave you with change from £30.

*18 Crawford Street, W1H 1BT
Nearest station: Marylebone
anothercountry.com @anothercountryltd*

28

NATIVE & CO

Simply beautiful Japanese homeware

This shop specialises in the 'quiet and functional', the sort of things that make a room feel more pulled together, even if they're not immediately noticeable. Think bath stools in creamy Japanese cyprus and wafer-thin bamboo bowls for mixing matcha. Taiwanese and British-Japanese owners Sharon Jo-Yun Hung and Chris Yoshiro Green travel to Japan several times a year to meet master craftsmen such as Takahiro Yagi, the sixth generation of his family to make traditional Kaikado tea caddies. Without their personal connections, these works of art would never make it to this side of the Pacific.

116 Kensington Park Road, W11 2PW
Nearest station: Notting Hill Gate
nativeandco.com @nativeandco

29

THE SPICE SHOP

Seasoning emporium for serious foodies

This mustard-yellow shop has been tempting top chefs to Portobello Market since 1995. It may be barely bigger than a restaurant's pantry, but the stock reads like a road map of the ancient spice routes: ground cinnamon from Ceylon, Lebanese thyme, potent French garlic and more than 18 types of chilli. Owner Birgit Erath grew up in Germany's Black Forest, where she spent her childhood foraging wild herbs with her grandmother and mixes the spice blends herself. They vary from batch to batch, but the personal touch makes them all the more covetable. And with her stock turning over so quickly, you always come away with the freshest and most aromatic of ingredients.

1 Blenheim Crescent, W11 2EE
Nearest station: Ladbroke Grove
thespiceshop.co.uk @thespiceshoplondon

30

LEILA'S SHOP

Shoreditch's village grocer

One of Leila McAlister's favourite childhood memories is going to the greengrocer with her dad and there's an appealing air of nostalgia about her shop's Victorian counter and original wooden panelling. However, her approach to provenance couldn't be fresher. The lighting is low to keep fruit and veg cool, while grains and dried goods are sold without packaging where possible to allow them to breathe. Rare varieties of peach, pear and plum produced in partnership with small growers are on offer to lucky east Londoners prepared to pay a little extra for the best on the market. Linger over Leila's signature dish of fried eggs with sage at the adjoining café.

15–17 Calvert Avenue, E2 7JP
Nearest station: Shoreditch High Street
leilasshop.co.uk @leilas_shop

31

EASTERN BIOLOGICAL

Gift shop inspired by natural history

It was while studying at Brighton University that Alfred Addis hatched the dream of a haven where nature-loving city dwellers could immerse themselves in natural history. The result feels like a cross between an eccentric professor's study and east London gift shop. Mossy panels line the walls, intriguing algae balls bob in glass jars and an aging labrador called Abra sports a zebra-print bandana as she snoozes in the corner. Downstairs, flick through beautiful nature-themed children's books and outdoorsy magazines; upstairs, browse garden-inspired gifts sure to get budding Monty Dons as enthused as the sight of a perfectly pruned perennial.

485 Hackney Road, E2 9ED
Nearest station: Cambridge Heath
easternbiological.co.uk @easternbiological

32

ARTWORDS

The last word on contemporary visual arts

No matter what time you arrive at this Shoreditch bookshop, there'll probably be at least one well-dressed creative looking for inspiration. Tables and shelves are stacked high with books and hard-to-get magazines from around the world – browse glossy coffee table tomes on Kyoto's tiniest buildings, collections of flyers from New York's rave scene and artist-written works on fashion, graphic design and architecture published by Artwords' own press. Hungry for more? The larger Broadway market site is a 25-minute walk.

69 Rivington Street, EC2A 3AY
Nearest station: Old Street
Other location: London Fields
artwords.co.uk @artwordsbookshop

33

DIY ART SHOP

A playfully curated hub for emerging artists

The sign outside promises 'zines, prints, originals and ceramics' but in reality this snug shop carries so much more. Owner Mark Farhall runs pop-up art markets where emerging names can showcase their work, before cherry-picking the most exciting. The space feels like a working studio thanks to its no-frills fitout. Enjoy a window installation by local artists before browsing planters illustrated with amusing slogans, as well as risograph prints from as far afield as Chile. See something you like? Snap it up – there are only ever a handful of each item. Turn to the back of the book for a short Q&A with Mark.

129 Shacklewell Lane, E8 2EB
Nearest station: Hackney Downs
diyartmarket.com @diyartshoplondon

34

PELICANS AND PARROTS

Designer vintage clothing and colourful
curios for your home

This colourful shop has been telling the stories of its owners since 2010. Hand-carved African masks studded with shells nod to Ochuko Ojiri's Nigerian heritage, while golden palm trees and feathered headdresses speak to Juliet Da Silva's sunshiney St Vincent background. The clothes are all sourced in Italy and tend to be the originals that inform today's trends: think ditsy 90s dresses, Fendi bags and big, bold Versace prints from the 80s. Beautiful things you don't need but are sure to want include Art Deco decanters in bonbon pink and shell hair clips from South Africa. Turn to the back of the book for a Q&A with Juliet.

40 Stoke Newington Road, N16 7XJ
Nearest station: Dalston Kingsland
pelicansandparrots.com @pelicansandparrots

35

PRICK

London's first dedicated cactus shop

From its cheeky name to the fact it was founded by someone with a background in forensic science rather than botany, everything about this shop is bold. Inspired by a visit to the Chelsea Flower Show, founder Gynelle Leon then spent a year researching cacti and travelling across America's deserts to see them in their natural habitat. She personally chooses every specimen, prioritising those with particularly interesting shapes and plenty of character. Gynelle also runs grafting workshops where you can learn to propagate new plants, and designs terracotta pots with modern, urban homes in mind. It's your one-stop shop for the kind of prick you actually want to live with.

492 Kingsland Road, E8 4AE
Nearest station: Dalston Junction
prickldn.com @prickldn

36

LABOUR AND WAIT

Utilitarian homewares with a design edge

For more than 20 years this shop has been on a mission to prove world-class design can make life's tedious chores that bit more beautiful. Sori Yanagi kettles sit beside Edwardian marmalade jars, pleasing scrubbing brushes jostle for space with Reiss enamel lamps, while dead-stock French workwear will have you itching to dig out your toolkit. Through their dedication to quality, owners Rachel Wythe-Moran and Simon Watkins act as the cool godparents of British crafts on the brink of extinction. Without their support, handmade jumpers from Guernsey and Welsh blankets as comforting as a hot bath might have quietly faded away.

85 Redchurch Street, E2 7DJ
Nearest station: Shoreditch High Street
labourandwait.co.uk @labourandwaitlondon

37

SCP

The godfather of east London design shops

In Shoreditch, design stores come and go, but SCP has been a Curtain Road constant for more than 30 years. It takes a lot to stay relevant in London's design mecca but SCP has it all: impeccable credentials in its founder Sheridan Coakley; three floors of furniture and accessories, many exclusive to the brand; and its own upholstery factory in Norfolk, where it crafts fabrics for furnishings by some of the biggest names in British design (yes Matthew Hilton, we're looking at you).

135–139 Curtain Road, EC2A 3BX
Nearest station: Old Street
scp.co.uk @scpltd

38

HOXTON MONSTER SUPPLIES

Fantastical novelty gifts to feed the imagination

Do you identify as human or monster? It's not a question one grapples with often but in this magical slither of Hoxton the only rule is to expect the extraordinary. Founded to raise funds for children's writing charity Ministry of Stories, the brainchild of author Nick Hornby, it sells the likes of human snot (which tastes surprisingly like lemon curd), tins of terror for monsters who've lost their mojo, and death certificates – because it never hurts to be prepared, right? The team of theatrical volunteers who run it make it an absolute joy to visit, no matter your age. Watch out for Wells, the shop's invisible cat, who you may hear meowing from time to time.

159 Hoxton Street, N1 6PJ
Nearest station: Hoxton
monstersupplies.org @monstersupplies

39

A NEW TRIBE

*Globally-gathered objects and textiles
with a difference*

Not only does owner Ella Jones curate this beautiful shop's stock, she also collaborates with artists to create special pieces for the home. From exclusive Sophie Alda ceramics to vases studded with fragments of objet d'art that were smashed in transit on their way to the shop, A New Tribe is filled with one-off pieces to give your home that Instagram edge. Located in a Victorian butcher's co-op with an original panelled ceiling, this airy site has the atmosphere of a gallery – except here ruffling that shaggy Azilal rug from Morocco is actively encouraged. Turn to the back of the book for a short Q&A with Ella.

*273 Hackney Road, E2 8NA
Nearest station: Cambridge Heath
anewtribe.co.uk @anewtribe*

40

THE MERCANTILE

Contemporary threads curated by stylish staff

With 150 independent brands and a passionate, impeccably dressed team, this shop has more in common with the Spitalfields Market traders of yesteryear than the high street giants who dominate the area today. Rather than blindly following trends, stock is informed by a seasonal theme such as 'Italian Riviera', or one of founders Debra and Thomas McCann's favourite films. The results are eclectic – including names such as Cus, Armedangels and Native Youth – with price points ranging from £30 to £300. Go in with an open mind and you'll come out with a fresh new look. Note the wooden till, which has been on the premises for more than a century.

17 Lamb Street, E1 6EA
Nearest station: Liverpool Street
themercantilelondon.com @mercantilelondon

41

NOBLE FINE LIQUOR

Hip bottle shop specialising in natural pours

If you drink oat milk and wear round spectacles, chances are you already know Broadway Market's best liquor shop. It's owned by the team behind east London restaurants Bright and P. Franco, and has a similar simple-yet-sophisticated feel. All wines are produced organically or biodynamically by small producers, mostly in France and Italy, although there are a few rising stars from Australia and Germany (including the Brand brothers). It's the kind of bottle shop every 20-something with a little extra cash needs at the end of their street. Nearly the end of the month? Bottles on the middle table are all £20 and under.

27 Broadway Market, E8 4PH
Nearest station: Cambridge Heath
noblefineliquor.co.uk @noblefineliquor

42

KILL THE CAT

Unusual craft beers in a crisp setting

With its birch parquet flooring and custom-built tasting block, this bar-shop hybrid has more than a whiff of Scandinavia about it. Owners Phil Curl and Wes Anson own a design company and were determined to lift London's craft beer scene out of the 'bro-ey', bearded place it was languishing in in 2016. Manager Dan Sandy is a certified cicerone (beer sommelier) and is always on hand to guide you through their 150-strong collection. Grab a takeaway from Brick Lane, pull out a stool and crack open a cold one.

43 Brick Lane, E1 6PU
Nearest station: Aldgate East
killthecat.co.uk @killthecatbeer

43

PHLOX BOOKS

An inviting spot for books and booze

After falling in love with the bar-bookshop hybrids of Le Marais while living in Paris, Aimée Madill was determined to create a similar feeling in Leyton. Unlike London's many more rarified bookshops, Phlox is a true community space. Aimee's three children run in and out throughout the day, while evenings see freelancers sipping Allpress coffee replaced by local literature-lovers perusing the shelves, glass of wine in hand. Titles veer towards the quirky and less-discovered rather than commercial bestsellers. With daily deliveries, there's always a reason to come back.

159 Francis Road, E11 4BS
Nearest station: Leyton
phloxbooks.com @phloxbooks

44

SEARCH & RESCUE

Eclectic homewares and gifts from indie brands

Whether looking for that perfect mid-century sofa or a new scent, you're sure to find something irresistible at one of Stokey's most popular lifestyle stores. Sniff a huge selection of craft candles before ogling the ceramics case, which includes treasures from London talent Jode Pankhurst. There are a great range of price points too. Whether you've found a forgotten fiver or are looking to invest in a graphic throw from Slowdown Studio, it's impossible to leave this shop empty-handed. Consider yourself warned.

129 Stoke Newington Church Street, N16 0UH
Nearest station: Stoke Newington
searchandrescuelondon.co.uk
@searchandrescuelondon

45

MELROSE AND MORGAN

Modern-day grocer specialising in artisan products

Named after the founders' respective mothers, this shop is as warm and wholesome as their home-cooked meals. Visiting Borough Market was a weekend ritual for Ian James and Nick Selby in the early 00s and they were determined to capture that authenticity in their Primrose Hill shop. Stock up on seasonal British produce – salmon from Secret Smokehouse, gourmet sauces by The Grocer on Elgin and organic fruit – before rewarding yourself with a break in their on-site café. Fingers crossed the house-made fish finger sandwich with crunchy slaw is on the menu for your visit.

42 Gloucester Avenue, NW1 8JD
Nearest station: Chalk Farm
Other location: Hampstead Heath
melroseandmorgan.com @melroseandmorgan

46

HUB

Fresh threads and friendly service

It may stock hip east London designers LF Markey and Kate Sheridan, but Hub is a clothes shop sewn from old-fashioned values. It's the sort of place where the team deliver to local customers on bicycle and end up stopping for a cuppa at every other house. For nearly 20 years sisters Georgie Cook and Louise Power have been dressing the residents of Stoke Newington and beyond, giving as much shelf space to first-time designers as international names like Ganni. Browse Japanese socks, illustrated cards and French perfume while chatting with ultra-friendly staff, most of whom have been part of the Hub family for more than a decade. London rarely makes shops like this anymore.

49 Stoke Newington Church Street, N16 0AR
Nearest station: Stoke Newington
hubshop.co.uk @hubshop_online

47

INSIDESTORE

*A light-hearted collection of contemporary
furniture and homewares*

The only criteria for what's featured in this eclectic
shop is that owner Andrea Bates must personally love
it. She honed her eye for detail during an early career
buying for Heals and Paperchase and you can see her
modern, relaxed taste in everything from £3 cacti to
£3,000 Outline sofas. Join Tufnell Park's locals in
browsing furniture from mostly European brands such
as Copenhague, HAY and Hartô, or search for the
perfect housewarming gift among her collection of
kooky accessories. Pair of ceramic planters shaped like
feet, anyone?

*155–157 Fortress Road, NW5 2HR
Nearest station: Tufnell Park
insidestoreldn.com @insidestoreldn*

48
KITCHEN PROVISIONS

Creative kitchen kit with a story

You may not know how much you need a gyuto knife until you stumble across it in this Victoriana-inspired shop. Knife specialists Tom Saunders and Helen Symmonds met whittler Jake Knibbs while working at markets, and the three set out to create a chaotic temple to kitchen craft. Pull open the drawers of antique butchers' blocks to stumble on ox tongue pressers, wasabi graters and squid clips, or take your pick from more than 200 Japanese knives which glint behind the counter. Symmonds lived in Japan for several years, and her personal relationships with makers means they have blades that can't be found anywhere else in the UK.

136 Stoke Newington Church Street, N16 0JU
Nearest Station: Stoke Newington
Other location: King's Cross
kitchenprovisions.co.uk @kitchenprovisions

49

BLACKHORSE LANE ATELIERS

London's only craft jean maker

Second-generation tailor Bilgehan Ates has cloth in his blood – the Ates family ran manufacturing factories across east London. Today, his handmade jeans brand is still firmly rooted in his family's adopted city. Every style is made on-site with quality denim from Japan, Turkey or Italy and is named after a local postcode. The central display cabinet is carved from a London plane tree that originally towered above Euston Station. With prices approaching £200 per item you won't be popping in for a new outfit too often, but when the workmanship is this good you don't need to.

Unit 32 Lower Stable Street, N1C 4DQ
Nearest station: King's Cross St Pancras
Other location: Walthamstow
blackhorselane.com @blackhorselane

50

MOLLY MEG

Design-led children's store

The butcher, baker and grocer on Essex Road have all been there for more than 30 years and, with its tapestry kits and wooden toys, Molly Meg feels equally timeless, despite only opening in 2015. Look out for dreamy Ibiza brand Numero 74 which sells linen dolls' clothes handmade by vulnerable women in Thailand. Free Sunday art workshops led by owner Molly Price and other guest creatives give you a few hours to mooch in Islington's boutiques while your mini Matisse creates a masterpiece.

111 Essex Road, N1 2SL
Nearest station: Essex Road
*mollymeg.com @molly_meg_*

51

PAPER MACHE TIGER

*Luxury fashion and a smattering
of chic home accessories*

With the fashion communications arm of the company located on site, Paper Mache Tiger staff are uniquely placed to understand the fashion world from within and without. The originality of the stock, from a combination of up-and-coming designers and classic European labels, reflects their expertise, while the site itself is spectacular. This former pencil factory's glass gables bring to mind a hothouse, except here you'll find colourful clothes by Allude, Petar Petrov and Eudon Choi, rather than flowers. Founder Kyle Robinson studied fine art and his own brand, Être Cécile, is a must for anyone who loves statement graphics.

26 Cross Street, N1 2BG
Nearest station: Essex Road
papermachetiger.com @papermachetigershop

52

WORD ON THE WATER

New and used books on a 1920s Dutch barge

This barge's motley crew comprises Cornishman Paddy Screech, artist and anarchist Jon Privett and a parrot called Jasper, who makes the noise of a police siren when feeling unappreciated. Bags of books arrive at the door almost daily, donations from Londoners who no doubt adore their stroll along the towpath to this Carrolian wonderland. Enjoy a particularly good selection of contemporary non-fiction and cult American classics (loitering for a moment by the log burning stove), before heading outside to catch live poetry performances on the roof.

Regent's Canal Towpath, N1C 4LW
Nearest station: King's Cross St Pancras
wordonthewater.co.uk @word_on_the_water

53
TWENTYTWENTYONE

Pared-back modern design classics

A wander around Islington's most lauded interiors shop is a lesson in contemporary design. Founders Tony Cunningham and Simon Alderson have been on the scene since 1996 and act as mentors for young designers, as well as collaborating with more established names like DK3, and furnishing large swathes of the Barbican. There's plenty of representation from the Danish and Japanese schools, as well as light-hearted touches such as hand-carved crow sculptures from artist Mikael Nilsson. Anything bought here is sure to be in good taste and built to last.

274–275 Upper Street, N1 2UA
Nearest station: Angel
Other location: Clerkenwell
twentytwentyone.com @twentytwentyone

54

WHAT MOTHER MADE

Unisex children's clothes made by hand

This delightful children's label began life as a stall on Broadway Market and craftsmanship and community are still its guiding principles. All the garments are made at their Well Street site by east London seamstresses, with minimal waste of fabrics. There is a fitting service at their newer Stokey site – if the garment is anything but perfect they'll alter it for no extra cost. Founder Charlotte Denn sees success as creating 'something special enough to become a hand-me-down', and her traditional shapes in modern fabrics, including African print, are timeless. If only mother made bigger sizes for grown-ups too.

166 Stoke Newington Church Street, N16 0JL
Nearest station: Stoke Newington
Other location: Homerton
whatmothermade.co.uk @whatmothermade

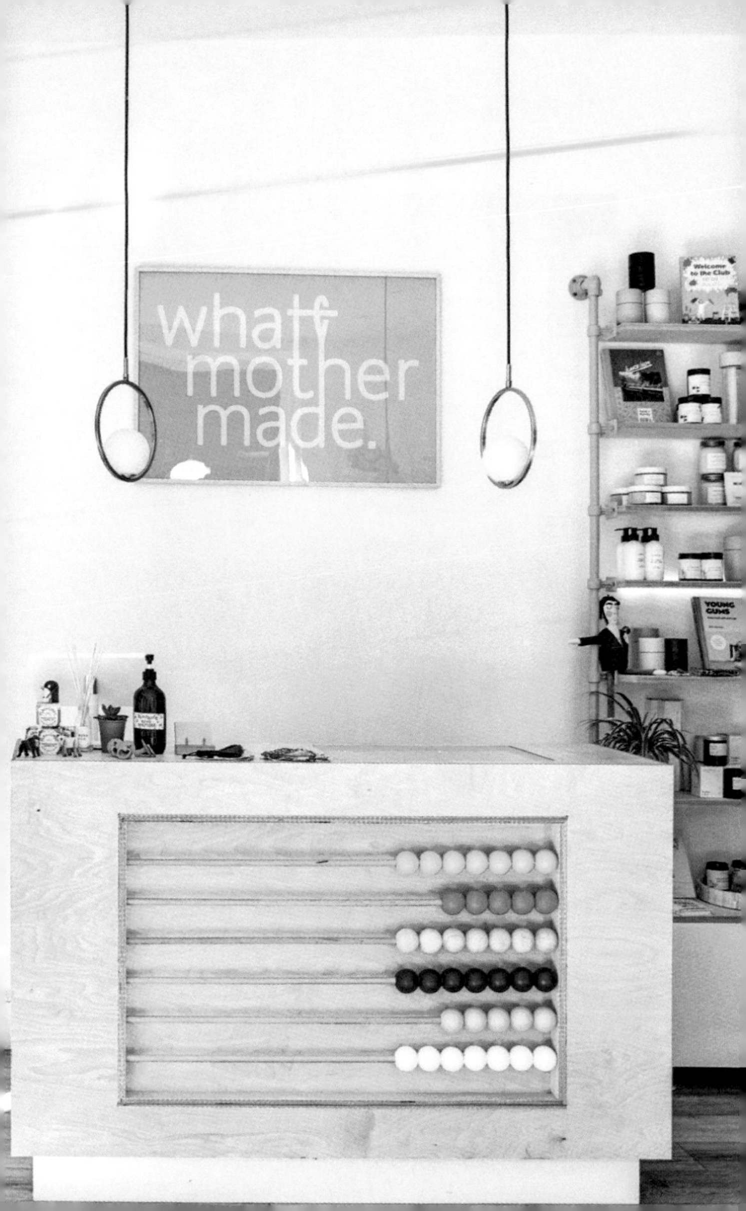
what mother made.
Welcome to the Club
YOUNG GUMS

ELLA JONES

A New Tribe (no.39)

What can indie shops offer that the high street can't? Independent shops offer a more personal experience. Each one is unique as it is often the owner's curation, selection and vision. They are generally run by a small team of like-minded people who really know and value each object. There's a sense of community among the staff and customers, and also through the pieces that are stocked and the people who make them.

Why do you think there has been a revived interest in independent shops? I think people are feeling more of an ethical responsibility when shopping now. There is definitely a shift away from the mass produced towards craft and knowing the story of each object. Independent shops inherently support this ethos. While devastating for many businesses, the Coronavirus pandemic has made people much more aware of supporting shops in their own community. The support has been really touching.

What do you think the future of the high street will look like? It's hard to predict the full impact of online shopping, but I feel there's a strong appetite for experience-led physical spaces. Hopefully in the long run this will lead to more diverse high streets which resonate with the communities around them.

MARK FARHALL

DIY Art Shop (no.33)

How do your personal interests influence your shop? My stock is informed by my background in illustration and fine art drawing, as well as my interest in counter culture, ephemera and abstract art. I love artists who show an innovative, adventurous approach to their practice. My choice of stock is self-indulgent, as I pick artwork that I'd like to make or take home.

What part do independent shops play in supporting small makers? My shop supports a diverse community of creatives by exposing them to a wider audience which increases their sales, therefore enabling their practice to be sustainable. I regularly collaborate with artists on exclusive items and host exhibitions where they can network and display their recent projects. Facilitating these pop-up events is creatively satisfying for me and in turn increases interest in the shop.

What do you think the future of the high street will look like? DIY Art Shop is on a quiet street that has very little passing foot-fall. The majority of our customers are enthusiastic followers of our Instagram account. When they visit, many share photos to support us and the artists we represent. I think this organic, consumer-led growth is how independent shops will continue to thrive.

JULIET DA SILVA

Pelicans and Parrots (no.34)

Why did you start your own business? I've lived in Dalston for many years and around 2010 noticed an influx of young creatives. The night-time culture was thriving, but there wasn't much to cater for them during the day so I saw a gap in the market. Our idea was a dream wardrobe coupled with beautiful objects. It's very much like a personal collection that's actually for sale.

How do you select your stock? We choose all the items ourselves and 95% of our vintage clothes are sourced from Italy. I travel there regularly and handpick every item. My background in textiles means that strong patterns often inform my choices, along with classic design and construction. I also buy a lot of designer 90s labels such as Versace, Moschino and Missoni. The homewares are sourced from all over Europe and beyond. We only buy what we love and would display in our own home.

What kind of relationship do you have with your customers? Being an owner-operator really allows you to connect with repeat customers. We make a point of getting to know what many of our regulars want and this helps provide more of a bespoke experience. If they have a particular outfit in mind, we'll source individual items for them.

SHOPS BY TYPE

An Opinionated Guide to Independent London
First edition

Published in 2020 by Hoxton Mini Press, London
www.hoxtonminipress.com
Copyright © Hoxton Mini Press 2020. All rights reserved.

Text by Imogen Lepere
Photography © Lesley Lau*
Copy-editing by Faith McAllister
Design by Daniele Roa
Production by Anna De Pascale
Production and editorial support by Becca Jones

*except images for Twentytwentyone © Twentytwentyone; Prick
© Jon Devo; London Terrariums (excluding portrait) © Rick Pushinsky;
Present and Correct (pages following main text spread) © Present and Correct

With thanks to Matthew Young for initial series design
and to our Kickstarter backers who invested in our future:
Andrew, Laura and Raphael Beaumont, Anonymous,
David Rix, Don McConnell, Duncan, Liss and Theo, Fiona and
Gordon (Bow), Gareth Tennant, Gary, Graham McClelland, Herlinde,
Jenifer Roberts, Jennifer Barnaby, Joe Skade, Jonathan Crown,
Jonathan J. N. Taylor, Matt Jackson, Melissa O'Shaughnessy, Nigel S,
Rob Phillips, Rory Cooper, Simon Robinson and Steev A. Toth

ISBN: 978-1-910566-82-4

Printed and bound by OZGraf, Poland